Take a trip to
JAMAICA

Keith Lye

Franklin Watts

London   New York   Sydney   Toronto

Facts about Jamaica

Area:
10,991 sq. km
(4,224 sq. miles)

Population:
2,288,000

Capital:
Kingston

Largest cities:
Kingston (525,000)
Spanish Town (89,000)
Montego Bay (70,000)
May Pen (41,000)
Mandeville (35,000)

Official language:
English

Religion:
Christianity, Rastafarian

Main exports:
Bauxite and alumina,
sugar, bananas, fruits

Currency:
Jamaican dollar

Franklin Watts
12a Golden Square
London W1

Franklin Watts Inc.
387 Park Avenue South
New York, N.Y. 10016

ISBN: UK Edition 0 86313 719 9
ISBN: US Edition 0 531 10558–X
Library of Congress Catalog
Card No: 87-51701

Typeset by Ace Filmsetting Ltd.,
Frome, Somerset
Printed in Hong Kong

© Franklin Watts Limited 1988

Maps: Simon Roulstone

Design: Pritilata Chauhan

Stamps: Harry Allen International
Philatelic Distributors

Photographs: Anne Bolt, 4, 5, 6, 7, 12, 13,
16, 17, 19, 20, 21, 24, 25, 27, 28, 29; Chris
Fairclough, 8; Hutchison Library, 14, 15,
18, 23, 26, 31; Rex Features, 10; Zefa, 3,
11, 22
Front Cover: Anne Bolt
Back Cover: Jamaica Tourist Board

Jamaica is a beautiful country. It is the third largest island in the West Indies. Its name comes from the word Xaymaca. This was the name used by the American Indians who lived there when the explorer Christopher Columbus claimed the island for Spain in 1494.

Jamaica's best known resort is Montego Bay. It is often called Mobay for short. It has magnificent sandy beaches. Montego Bay is Jamaica's third largest town, after the capital Kingston and Spanish Town.

Several impressive waterfalls are found near the resort of Ocho Rios on the north coast. Dunn's River Falls drops more than 200 m (656 ft) down a series of steps. People bathe in the pools on the steps.

Jamaica has many short rivers, such as the Morant River in the southeast. The highlands in this picture are the Blue Mountains. They contain Jamaica's highest point, Blue Mountain Peak, which is 2,256 m (7,402 ft) high.

Jamaica has a tropical climate. Temperatures on the coast are high throughout the year, although the Blue Mountain region is much cooler. The rainfall varies from about 80 cm to more than 200 cm (31–79 inches).

The picture shows some stamps and money used in Jamaica. The main unit of currency is the Jamaican dollar, which is divided into 100 cents.

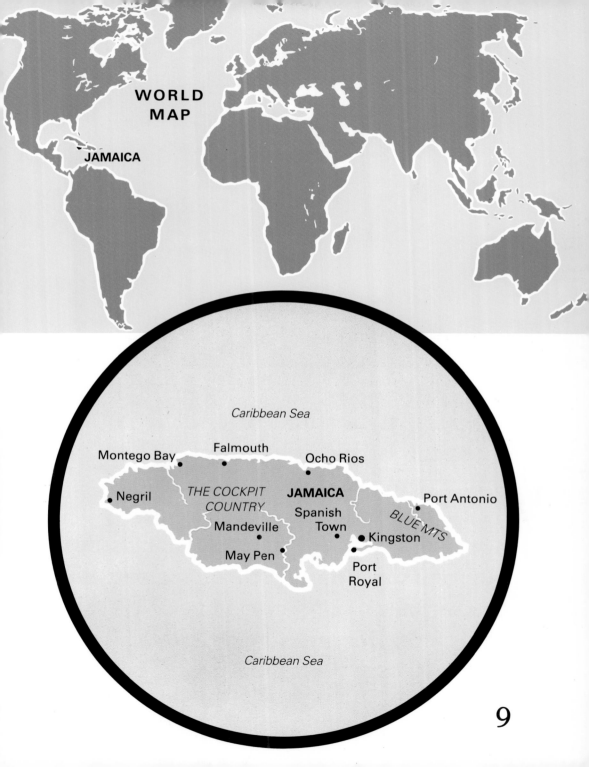

WORLD MAP

JAMAICA

Caribbean Sea

Montego Bay Falmouth Ocho Rios

Negril *THE COCKPIT COUNTRY* **JAMAICA** Port Antonio

Spanish Town *BLUE MTS*

Mandeville Kingston

May Pen

Port Royal

Caribbean Sea

Spain ruled Jamaica until 1655
when the British invaded it. British
forces controlled most of the island
by 1660. In the 1670s, Port Royal
became a base for pirates, such as Sir
Henry Morgan. The pirates attacked
Spanish ships and ports in the West
Indies. An earthquake destroyed
much of Port Royal in 1692.

Spanish Town, 20 km (12 miles) west of Kingston, was founded in the 1520s by the son of Christopher Columbus. It was the capital of Jamaica until 1872. The old town centre, shown in this picture, resembles the squares in many old towns in Spain.

Kingston was founded in 1693 after the destruction of Port Royal. It became the island's commercial capital in 1703 and the national capital in 1872. It was severely damaged by an earthquake in 1907. About half of the people of Jamaica live in the cities and towns.

Jamaica became independent in 1962. It became a monarchy, with Britain's Queen as its Head of State. The Queen is represented in Jamaica by a Governor-General who lives in the house seen below. The prime minister is the head of the government.

The original people of Jamaica, the Arawak Indians, died out through disease and overwork by the early 16th century. The Spaniards brought in black slaves from Africa. Some of their descendants, called Maroons, fought against British rule. Britain signed a peace treaty with the Maroons in 1738.

Today, more than 90 per cent of Jamaicans are of African or mixed African and European descent. There are also some people of Asian and European descent. The official language is English, but most people speak a dialect which Americans and Britons often find hard to understand.

The Spaniards introduced Roman
Catholicism into Jamaica. But today
most people are Protestants, including
Anglicans and Baptists. The picture
shows part of the old cathedral in
Spanish Town. This cathedral was
built in the 15th century.

Some Jamaicans, such as Canute Thompson, a sculptor, shown here, are Rastafarians. They got their name from Ras Tafari. This was the original name of the former Emperor of Ethiopia, Haile Selassie I. Rastafarians believe that Haile Selassie was God.

Bauxite mining is Jamaica's leading industry. Jamaica is the world's third most important bauxite producer. Gypsum and silica are also mined in Jamaica.

18

Several factories process bauxite, turning it into a substance called alumina. Bauxite and alumina make up about two-thirds of the value of Jamaica's exports.

Cigarettes are one of the items made in factories in the towns. Other manufactures include cement, chemicals, processed foods, and various petroleum products. The petroleum is imported and processed in a refinery in Kingston.

Farming employs 31 per cent of the workforce, as compared with 16 per cent in industry and 52 per cent in services, such as tourism. The leading crop is sugar cane. Some of the sugar is used to make molasses (a thick treacle) and rum.

Bananas are another major crop in Jamaica. Farmers also produce citrus fruits, cocoa and coffee. In recent years, the government has encouraged the production of new things, including flowers, honey and winter vegetables.

Some rice is grown as a food crop, together with cassava, coconuts, maize (corn), potatoes and yams. But there is not enough farm produce in Jamaica to feed its people. As a result, much food has to be imported.

Crops are grown on 21 per cent of the land in Jamaica, while grazing land covers another 23 per cent. Cattle, raised for beef and dairy products, are the leading animals. Goats, pigs and poultry are also important.

Tourism brings in more foreign
money to Jamaica than any activity
other than the bauxite and alumina
exports. Much money has been spent
on building new resorts and hotels.
This hotel is at Falmouth, to the east
of Montego Bay.

Jamaica has private nursery schools for children whose parents can afford to pay fees. Most children start school at the age of six. Most go to free elementary schools. Three out of every four Jamaicans can read and write.

Education is compulsory for children between the ages of six and sixteen. Secondary education in government-aided schools is also free, but less than half of the children of secondary school age actually attend school.

The University of the West Indies is near Kingston. In the mid-1980s, it had more than 4,000 students. Jamaica also has teacher training colleges, a College of Arts, Science and Technology, and a College of Agriculture.

People who live in towns are generally more prosperous than those who live in the country. Popular dishes in Jamaica include pepperpot (a thick soup), rice and peas seasoned with onions and coconut milk, and jerk pork (spicy slices of pork).

Jamaica is famous for its music,
especially reggae, which began there.
Reggae is a type of music which
blends African drum rhythms,
American rhythm and blues and
modern electric guitars.

Most people like sports. Cricket, a popular team game, is a reminder of Jamaica's close ties with Britain. The picture shows a match between the West Indies and England at Kingston's Sabina Park.

Index